Spec·Fi

101 Fantasy

Writing Prompts

Volume 1

J. Dodson

SpecFicWrit: 101 Fantasy Writing Prompts, Volume 1

ISBN 13: 978-1515012733

ISBN 10: 1515012735

To the Dreamers
To the Creators
To the Challengers
To the Explorers

We Choose Our Fate,
Just as Our Fate Chooses Us.
Though We May Not Set Out to,
We are the Changers of Worlds.
For We are Never Satisfied,
Always Seeking to Answer the Unanswerable
What If.

Table of Contents

GETTING STARTED...

This book will not teach you how to write. Nor will it show you how to become a better writer.

It may help you along those paths. But it will not illustrate the way.

It is a match, not a map.

This is Not a "How-To" Book

There are no rules here.

A few tricks of the trade? Perhaps. A few examples? Of course. Thoughts, ideas, strategies? Most certainly.

There are no exercises here. No "story starter" sentences to follow. No pre-established plot points. The only limitations set within these pages are the ones you place upon yourself and your imagination.

This book is not a guide. It is a tool. It won't teach you. But it may help you teach yourself.

It is a key. Use it to unlock the creative genius within.

It is a match. Use it to ignite ideas from the depths of your psyche.

How well it works is up to you and how you choose to wield it.

I make one promise. The more you use it, the better at using it you will become.

No one picks up a sword for the first time and knows how to brandish it like an expert. No one takes up the violin and becomes a master the moment they place bow upon strings. It takes time. Effort. Dedication. Discipline.

The sword is a tool of war and defense. The violin is a tool of music and beauty. This book is a tool for exposing unhindered imaginings, drawing them from the soul to the page.

Like all great endeavors, writing requires practice. That is how this book will help you. With it, you will practice. You will grow. You will develop. With it, you may learn about yourself, your craft, your strengths, and your weaknesses.

Whatever you glean is up to you.

Methods and Madness

What are Prompts?

In a nutshell, prompts are simply words or phrases used to spark something within the imagination. Once you read your prompt, you write whatever comes to mind.

Simple as that.

Vague? A bit.

But in all honesty, how you write, how much you write, how often, and what you write is all up to you. The prompt is just the spark. How much it ignites and how long it burns is up to the writer.

Each prompt in this book was specifically chosen because it strikes the chord that is Fantasy. Whether you write about wizards, mermaids, magic, heroes, dragons, or animals wearing fashionable footwear, each prompt is a spark for the unlimited, unhindered genre of fantastical worlds, creatures, characters, and abilities.

There are many paths and trails within the grand land of Imagination. Which path you choose is up to you, and each day you might choose a different one. Will you go down the long and winding trail of historical fantasy? Or will you traverse the alternate reality just beyond our borders? Will you find yourself in an urban setting rife with illegal magic? Or will you be somewhere entirely unseen, a world of your own creation where anything, and everything is possible?

There are no right or wrong paths, just as there are no right or wrong ways to use this book. There are methods, some of which you'll find below. But those are merely suggestions. You must discover what works best for you.

Some writers work better with rigidity. Others thrive with fluidity. Some are a combination of the two. Some writers stick to the same method. Others mix it up. It all depends upon the individual.

Test the waters. Experiment. Find where you stand. And go from there.

And what better way to learn than to dive in and practice? If something doesn't work, try a different method. If something works, explore it. Develop it. Expand upon it.

When you find what works best, you may just find yourself writing uninhibited.

HOW OFTEN SHOULD YOU PRACTICE?

How often you practice is entirely up to you.

Some practice every day—and I suggest it. The more you do something, the more proficient you become at it.

Others practice as often as their lives allow. Though writing takes a backseat, those who practice as often as they can are at least making an effort to grow and develop.

Yet others practice only when the need or desire takes them. Instead of teaching the muse to waken inside them, they simply wait for it to do so on its own. It's a slow means of progression, if one progresses at all.

Whatever you decide, however you choose, keep in mind the more you write, the better a writer you will become. The more you welcome the muse to come to you, the more you will find it there ready and waiting to begin the grand adventure of uninhibited writing.

RANDOM VS PLANNED

When you open this book to the first page of prompts, you'll find a list of words or phrases. They'll be numbered. Use the numbers however you see fit. As a reference to a specific prompt. Or as a guideline to how you'll use the prompts and when.

The Planned Method:

Follow the list from one to one hundred and one. Or in reverse. You could pick the prompt at the top of each page until the pages end and then go back to the beginning for number two on each page, and so on. Or you could go through the list, picking and choosing what prompts strike you the most, and jotting each down on a calendar or schedule.

Planned simply means you know what your prompt will be ahead of time.

The Random Method:

Create a spinner. Roll the dice (a ten sided die works best for this). Close your eyes, flip through the book, and point. That is your prompt.

Random simply means you don't know what you'll write until you're ready to write.

❖ ❖ ❖ ❖ ❖ ❖ ❖

Both methods have their merits. Planned gives you time to think about what you want to write. Random leaves things to the imagination until the very moment pen touches paper (or fingers to keyboard). Some people work better when they have an established idea. Others find not knowing liberating.

TIMED VS COUNTS VS UNLIMITED

How much should you write for each prompt?

It all depends upon you. How much time can you devote to practice? How much creative energy do you have available for practice? What can you set aside?

However much you can devote, sometimes it helps to set goals.

Timed Goals

Time goals involve the use of stopwatches, music playlists, hourglasses, or anything that can be used to measure time. The entire point of timed goals is to establish a certain amount of time devoted solely to writing.

Write as much as you can within the allotted time. If you only get a couple of sentences out after an hour, that's okay. If you manage pages upon pages within only fifteen minutes, also okay. Just so long as you keep working throughout the span of time you set for yourself.

Count Goals

Word Count/Page Count goals don't involve time so much as space. You write for however long it takes to achieve your goal. A page. Half a page. Ten pages. Computers (and word processing programs) offer the grand opportunity of counting words in an instant. You could set your goal at 1000 words a day. Or 50,000 accumulative words in a month. You are your own gatekeeper.

Unlimited

Sometimes goals work well. And sometimes they can stifle. This is where the unlimited method comes in. No set times. No set counts. Just writing for as long and as much as the idea takes you. It could take you as far as five whole minutes of unhindered writing. Or it could take you as far as eight hours of losing yourself in your imagination. The only limit is you and what you are capable of.

STORIES VS SCENES VS SNIPPETS

What should you write? Should you write a whole story? Or just a part of a story? Should you do only beginnings? Or can you do endings and middles too?

Up to you.

Whole Stories

Whole stories involve beginnings, middles, and ends. If this comes easily to you, go for it. See where the stories take you. Each prompt could be its own story. Or each one could be a new scene in the same story. The possibilities are endless.

Scenes

If writing whole stories or continuing the same one each day seems too daunting, or if you simply don't know where you want an idea to take you, perhaps scenic prompts are more your speed. You could treat each prompt as a beginning to a new story. Or an ending. Or you could simply pick a place in the middle and go for it.

Scenes offer a bit more freedom. If you're writing somewhere in the middle of a story, details may already be established. You don't have to describe everything. It's already there, in the proverbial beginning. You don't have to set as much of the stage and you can focus more on one singular moment in the story.

Snippets

But what if you don't want either? What if you just have an idea? What if you don't know if it is even part of a story? Perhaps it's a bit of dialogue. Or a snapshot of some battle scene. Or an inner monologue. Or a sketch of a setting.

Ideas, bits, and pieces—these are snippets. Snippets offer the most freedom, but they also have the potential to be the shortest of the three. They can become stories, if expanded. They can be put into already established stories. Or they can be combined with other snippets to create something larger, grander, and completely unique.

✦ ✦ ✦ ✦ ✦ ✦ ✦

You don't have to stick to just one of the three. Embracing variety is embracing freedom. One day an idea might take you from beginning to the middle and eventually the end. The next day, perhaps all you can dream up is a conversation between an envelope and the pencil holder on your desk. The next day, you might be inspired to write a love scene in a sand-and-sandals style historical fantasy. Again, it all depends on you.

A Bit of Advice

Though there are no rules, regulations, rights, and wrongs, I do have one bit of advice to share.

Let go.

No matter what method you use, let go. Let go of expectations. Let go of the self. Let go and simply let the idea take you where it will. Let go of specificity. Let go of perfection. Let go of rules. Those can come later.

Prompts aren't about perfection. They're about practice. They're about developing the imagination, building skills, and creating a deeper connection between writer and the act of writing.

For now, the best piece of advice I can give is to simply let go and just write.

And sometimes, that is the most difficult thing to do.

How then, is it achieved? Like all other endeavors in life, through practice. The more you do it, the better at it you will be.

Before You Begin

Now that you have a general idea of how to use the tool that is this book, here are your **101 Prompts**. Actually, they begin in the next section. In the meantime, here are a few things to keep in mind before and after you delve in.

If you find these 101 prompts too easy, or too vague, take a look at the **Challenges** section where you'll find a list of 10 challenges to add a bit of flavor, difficulty, or clarity to your practice.

If you're unsure how to incorporate a challenge, take a look at the **Challenges Glossary** to get a better idea of what each one is and how they may apply to your writing.

At the back, you'll also find two **Helping Hands** sections:

Breaking the Block, Part 1: Stimulating the Senses

~and~

What Now? Part 1: The Art of Prompt Maturation

Both are parts of a series, and the continuations can be found in SPECFICWRIT 101 Fantasy Writing Prompts, Volumes 2, 3, and 4, the information for which you'll find in the last section of this book: **Not Quite the End.**

1O1 Sparks

Open to a blank page.

Write the date at the top.

Find your prompt.

Write it under the date.

Clear your mind.

Let go.

And write.

101 Fantasy Writing Prompts

1. Abject Poverty

2. Sprinkles

3. Underwater Caverns

4. Engravings

5. Ringlets Drifted to the Floor

6. River Stones

7. The Tome

8. Unlimited Wishes

9. Three's a Crowd

10. Haberdashery

11. Polarity

12. The Mask of Tragedy

73.   No, the Non-Fuzzy One

74.   Bow Before Your Rightful Ruler

75.   First Love

76.   Around the Campfire

77.   High in the Tunnel

78.   Duck

79.   Gifted

80.   Good and Bad Medicine

81.   Sweet Indulgences

82.   Coronation

83.   Shrinking

84.   Disgruntled

85.   They're Above Us

86.   Fair Trade

87.   Nomads

CHALLENGES

Every writer has one—that go to voice, style,
tense, or point of view that just flows naturally
from them. It's where they're their strongest,
where they feel most at home. And sometimes,
it's where they fall into a rut.

Sometimes, the best way to grow as a writer
is to face a challenge that shatters that
comfort zone.

Right and Wrong Do Not Apply

Challenges are exactly that—an added condition meant to challenge you, to test your skills and help you branch out of your comfort zone. A writer can only grow stronger the more they explore their craft and try new things. Though these challenges might seem basic, sometimes the best way to begin broadening one's horizons is to return to the fundamentals of the craft.

In this volume, all ten challenges center on Point of View (POV) and Tense. If you write primarily in First Person, you might find it challenging to try Third Person Omniscient. If you usually write from Protagonist's point of view, you might find it challenging to write a scene from the focus of your Antagonist. And what greater tense challenge is there than Future Tense?

Just like the prompts list, there's no right or wrong way to use the challenges list.

Roll a ten-sided dice. Or roll it twice. Spin a spinner. Ask someone for a number between one and ten. Deliberately choose one. Or close your eyes and point.

You might focus on one challenge at a time, using the same one throughout the week in order to truly get a feel for it. You might try a new one each day, mixing things up to keep you on your toes.

Or you could keep the same prompt title throughout the week, but try a different challenge each day, exploring which tenses and points of view work best for which ideas.

Another option is to combine challenges. Perhaps First Person, Future Tense is more your speed. Or you could try your hand at the Antagonist POV, Third Person Focused, Present Tense.

If you're unsure how to apply a challenge or what it means, remember to explore the Challenges Glossary where you'll find definitions and thoughts on each one.

POV and Tense Challenges

1. First Person

2. Second Person

3. Third Person Focused

4. Third Person Expanded

5. Third Person Omniscient

6. Past Tense

7. Present Tense

8. Future Tense

9. Protagonist POV

10. Antagonist POV

CHALLENGE GLOSSARY

Challenges are a means of growth. They provide the opportunity to develop new skills and find new strengths. By digging a little deeper, you'll plant your roots in richer soil.

The following pages aren't going to teach you how to write in each point of view and tense. After all, this isn't a how-to book.

Instead, you'll find hints, reminders, and thoughts, as well as samples and ideas for how you might apply the challenges to your own prompt writing.

First Person
(I, Me, Mine, Us, We, Ours)

First Person is considered one of the more personal and/or intimate of the various POV's. Typically, it allows the reader to delve directly into the mind of the character, as if living the character's life with them. It is limiting in that it only allows one perspective throughout the entire story, and interweaving subplots becomes more of a challenge. Nonetheless, it is one of the best POV's for reader immersion.

There are two different variations of the First Person POV: Singular and Plural. Most First Person fiction is written in singular form—I did, I went, I want, etc. However, it is possible, and perhaps an additional challenge, to write a story from a First Person Plural POV—we did, we went, we want.

EXAMPLE OF FIRST PERSON SINGULAR:

It was as far as I could go. A brick wall blocked my path, and my first thought was to turn around and retrace my steps. Sirens wailed from the next block, squashing the idea almost immediately. They were catching up.

I dismounted and dropped the bike at the side of the ally. It couldn't help me anymore. Staring at the wall, I reached into my pocket and pulled out the green crayon. It wasn't much more than a nub. Still, there might be just enough left.

The sirens howled all the louder, flashing blue and red reflecting off the wall. Someone said something over a loudspeaker, but I ignored it, pushing their proximity to the back of my mind. I needed to focus. I couldn't slip up now.

Concentration was key when drawing doors between the worlds. With so little crayon left, I needed all the concentration I could muster. More words shouted at me from the loudspeaker. I drew the first line. Feet slapped the wet pavement at the entrance to the alley. I drew the second. More officers arrived, completely blocking the alley. The third line took shape. One to go.

The sound of their weapons almost broke my concentration. My hand shook, knowing that at any moment they might use violence to stop me. I almost dropped the crayon, the nub now no bigger than the tip of my pinkie. But I didn't. I just managed to hold onto it long enough to complete the portal.

The streaks of green wax glowed and the four lines became a door. Just as the officers ran into the alley to stop me, I pushed open that door and dove through with little thought to where I might end up.

POSSIBLE INSTANCES OF FIRST PERSON PLURAL:

- ⅄ Someone who has (and is aware of) multiple personalities.
- ⅄ Someone who is possessed by one or more spirits.
- ⅄ One being with multiple heads.
- ⅄ Someone either controlling another's mind, or having their mind controlled.
- ⅄ Communal minds (similar to bees and ants)

EXAMPLES OF FIRST PERSON PLURAL:

Multiple Personalities

> We don't want the refugees here. What can we do but stare, knowing we're just as helpless as they are? Why can't they just go away? Let us be. Let us suffer alone. But no, they linger. In body and in our mind. Why can't we just not see them? Why can't we simply forget them?
>
> Our throat clenches, shutting off our voice before we can shout for them to leave us. A vice grips our heart, clenching our chest so that each breath we draw is agony. With shaking hands, we absently wipe sweat from our face and neck, our eyes locked on theirs. We can't turn away. Yet, we know there's nothing we can do. How can we hope to save them when we can't even save our self."

Possessed

> We are power. We are control. We are the stifling vice, the rancidness of his soul. We rot inside him; our putrid will is now his. He is ours. He will suffer. We will wrack his soul. He will do things because of us, unaware of us. He will become the horror we will him to be. He will lose himself to us, making room for more of us. We will fill him to overflowing. He will writhe in our wrath. Helpless. Hopeless.

Multiple heads

> Walking down the street, we struggled to ignore the stares, yet somehow found the will to hold our heads high. We forced ourselves to exude confidence. Confi-

dence in our existence, in our simultaneous individuality and duality. At least, we tried to. So what if we have two heads. Two minds are better than one. And in a way, were we any different than them? Many people are of two minds about something. We were just born to physically manifest this rather than internalize it.

Communal Minds

We heard the queen's command. And we obeyed. There was nothing but to obey. She was queen. She was all and everything. Undeniable. Yet, we didn't want to kill them. We didn't want to obey. How could we want anything when she is all? We were so confused. Yet, we obeyed.

◆ ◆ ◆ ◆ ◆ ◆ ◆

Another option is to combine both singular and plural as a means of showing character confusion. (If using this particular style, exercise caution. While you want the reader to feel the character's internal confusion, you don't want to actually confuse the reader.)

EXAMPLE OF COMBINING SINGULAR AND PLURAL

We wanted ice cream. No, I wanted. Not we. *We* wasn't real. It couldn't be real. I wouldn't believe it. I wouldn't give into it. Them. I wouldn't give into them. They didn't exist. Didn't they? Did I? Were they a part of me? Or was I a small part of their we? I couldn't deny us. We. Me. I didn't know. All I knew was we wanted ice cream.

Second Person

(You, Your, Yours)

Second Person is the least used POV in fiction. In most instances, it's primarily used as a device to tell a story about the reader themselves by means of an anonymous narrator. In other words, the narrator is in direct contact with the reader as opposed to being behind what many writers refer to as the "fourth wall."

Second Person can also be used as a means of delivering information about a character directly to that character. This second instance is most often seen in prophesies, fortune telling, predictions, etc.

EXAMPLES OF SECOND PERSON:

A character stumbles upon an ancient tome and reads about himself as if the events already happened (The tome is what is written in Second Person, though the rest of the story could be in a different POV. Often, though not always, this style of Second Person is written in Past Tense)

> He read on, unable to tear his eyes away and yet unable to fathom the text before him. It was real. It was him, his life, his deeds. It told of his very time in that labyrinth, the endless traps, tricks, secrets, clues, and puzzles, all intent on killing him. The words of the page floated past his eyes, unable to take hold for a moment.

How was this possible? Forcing himself to focus, he reread the last passage. And his heart practically stopped.

"My father, you didn't make it out of the maze. Though you survived several traps after reading this book, you just weren't strong enough to survive them all. Even when you read about your own demise, you knew then fighting it wouldn't change it. You knew you couldn't stop the inevitable. No one can change the past, present, or future. You accepted this, finished reading, and came to peace with the fate awaiting you. Despite knowing, you fought the next traps valiantly. You made it so far; you got so close to leaving the maze. Yet, a part of you had already died in this Chamber of Lost Futures. And that's what killed you. Not the trap. The knowledge. If only you hadn't read this. Yet, like all else, it was to be."

A character meets a prophet who enters her mind and mentally shares her fate. (Prophetic revelations and predictions are often—again not always—written in Future Tense)

You will marry him. And you'll have a child together. He will love you for all his days. Your daughter will be the best of both of you, his courage and your temperance.

But the war will rip your little family apart. You must be strong. You must be diligent and mustn't give in to the fear that will threaten to destroy you.

You will lose them, for a time or for all eternity, it is uncertain. One way or the other, it is up to you. If you find your faith and hold onto hope, then you'll survive.

> You'll all survive. If you cannot, you'll not only lose them forever, but also yourself.

A narrator "speaks" to the reader about the reader's journey from their mundane life into an alternate reality. (When the "fourth wall" is torn down and the reader has direct contact with the storyteller, it is most often done via Present Tense. This, however and like the above, is not set in stone.)

> You go down the stairs, each footfall carefully placed before the next one. You can't be too cautious; the stairs are treacherous. You don't want to trip and fall. Wishing for some light, you squint, trying to make out anything through the darkness. Are those shadows? Shapes? Solid forms or your own imagination? You don't know. All you know is you must keep going. You must make it to the bottom of the stairs. And from there... You're not sure. But you'll know when you get there.

Third Person

(He, Him, His, She, Her, Hers, It, Its, They, Them, Their, Theirs)

Third Person POV is one of the most prominent POV's in fiction and can be broken down in to various branches. Three of the more common branches are Focused, Expanded, and Omniscient.

Third Person Focused

Similar to First Person, Third Person Focused only deals with one character at a time. Of the three Third Person POV's, this one is the most intimate, but also the most limiting. While it allows readers to immerse themselves in a character, revealing the character's knowledge, thoughts, emotions, and motivations, it also limits the reader solely to that character's knowledge, thoughts, emotions, and motivations.

Third Person Focused lends itself well to scenic writing and what some writers call "head-hopping." Many authors use this POV to allow readers personal knowledge of multiple characters by using scene breaks to switch between character POV's.

If a writer head-hops between two different characters within a single scene, they are not writing in Third Person Focused. Focused is one character POV per scene. Other characters can be present, but the reader does not know anything about them other than what the POV character knows and/or observes.

If done right and transitioned well, this style of head-hopping allows the writer to intertwine various subplots with the main plot while also allowing readers to immerse themselves deeply in more than one character throughout a story.

An Example of Third Person Focused:

All three of her clients performed a superstitious act, each one as intriguing as it was pointless. Nonchalantly, yet not blatantly, she scanned them one by one, taking in any possibility of skill while at the same time observing their individual rituals. Too many years as a guide, she'd seen enough to recognize such superstitions for what they were. Futile. Meaningless. Pathetic.

One man stroked a rabbit's food. Poor bunny. Such an antiquated superstition, not to mention cruel. The rabbit's foot looked old. Much older than the man. Perhaps that's why he rubbed it so incessantly. Maybe it wasn't the foot so much as the previous owners.

Under the guise of checking their gear, she shifted her attention to the next man. This one muttered under his breath. Had she been fully human, she might not have made out the specifics of his gibberish. But then, had she been fully human, she wouldn't be leading them into the dangers beyond the gate.

His words were ritualistic nonsense, as were the repetitive actions that followed. Rise, kneel, rise, spin one way and then spin another, touch finger to forehead and then chest. Why? Why bother? How would such simple movements help him survive the paralyzing venom of the Splinter Arachnid? How could he believe such repetition would spare him the treacherously hypnotic beauty of the Cain Flowers? At least he inadvertently warmed up his body. It'd help during their first sprint.

No need to hide her curiosity with the last man. His ritual, whatever it was, required his eyes to be closed. But they weren't clenched. She tilted her head to the side, all of a sudden intrigued. How unusual. No one, in all her years as a guide, had ever exuded so much peace before venturing out into the wilderness. But why?

She let her eyes rove over his body. His health might be the key. Vital. Strong. Unlike the other two, he was in his prime, more than capable of caring for himself in an emergency. Yet, despite his obvious physical ability, he felt the need to perform a superstitious ritual. And like the confidence and peace radiating from him, she'd never encountered this particular ritual before.

He simply knelt upon one knee, one hand resting on his other knee for support. His other hand he placed over his heart. Like the second man, he muttered words to himself. She perked her ears and focused her attention completely on him. The words weren't for himself. They were for another. Yet, he wasn't speaking to anyone else in the room.

She looked away, curiosity now at war with genuine concern. Was he mad? Weak she could handle. Stupidity might be dangerous, but she could typically control those who exhibited it. But madness was beyond hazardous, especially in one as strong and physically capable as she was. In a fit, he might try to overpower her.

All thoughts and concerns diminished in an instant. The bells at the gate tower tolled, warning of the coming dawn. She gathered her things and prepared her mind. The two weak ones wouldn't be much of a problem as long as they obeyed her command. They didn't seem to have much ego to contend with, so no evident issues to be nipped in the bud that first day. She'd know more that night when they reached their first shelter.

The third man, however... She stole a glance, wary lest he see her. He rose, dusted off his knee, and looked boldly up at the gate, a trusting expression settled about his face and demeanor. No fear. None. And it wasn't due to foolishness, naivety, or false bravado.

Madness. She'd have to keep an eye on him.

Third Person Expanded

Third Person Expanded is the balance between Omniscient (all knowing) and Focused (one character at a time). Most often, the reader is allowed the knowledge, thoughts, emotions, and experiences of multiple characters at a time, but limited to those characters currently present in the scene.

Like Limited, it involves head-hopping. In this case, however, the hopping has no transition—it is seamlessly done between characters without having to switch scenes. Expanded offers the reader more information more readily. However, for the sake of experiencing more than one character at a time, the reader cannot immerse themselves as deeply into the characters as they could with First Person or Third Person Limited.

AN EXAMPLE OF THIRD PERSON EXPANDED:

Jane glanced at George, making eye contact before looking down, a coy smile teasing the corner of her lips. Embarrassed, she turned away to hide a blush. Had she really just tried one of Nancy's tricks? She wasn't a flirt. What was wrong with her?

Wanting to grin, George stifled the urge, knowing if he did it might add to her embarrassment. It might also encourage her current behavior, and he'd rather not. It was no mystery, Jane's feelings for him. But he couldn't fathom why she felt the need to act like Nancy in order to show him. She should just be herself. Even as he watched the blood rush to her face, he wondered at her actions. Half the time, she seemed genuinely sweet. The other half, she seemed nothing more than Nancy's puppet.

Bored, Terrence watched the entire exchange from the corner of his eye, willing one of them to finally make a move. Neither did, and he shook his head. Pathetic. Those two just needed to get it over with. And soon. Muttering as much loudly under his breath, he stormed between the two and left them and their awkward impotence in his dust. He thought to join Nancy walking at the head of their company, but slowed to walk behind her instead. He liked the view much better from back there.

Third Person Omniscient

Third Person Omniscient POV is the broadest of all the POV's. In essence, it is the story told by an all knowing, all seeing narrator who knows every character's thoughts, emotions, and motivations all at once regardless of their importance to the story or whether they're present at the moment. This narrator can share some, any, and/or all with the reader without transition or scene break.

Though head-hopping can occur in Third Person Omniscient, and though the narrator of the story can delve deeper/focus more intently on the primary characters of the story, the POV lends itself to a much more expansive, world-wide scale.

Prologues and backstories are often written in Third Person Omniscient, regardless of whether the main story is or not. In this way, the narrator can focus more on events as they affect the world as a whole rather than how they affect individual characters or smaller groups of characters.

AN EXAMPLE OF THIRD PERSON OMNISCIENT:

Blue Frost. It was the beginning. And it was the end. It brought life, light, and beauty. And it wrought death, destruction, and decay. One simple crystal, one bit of magic. So benign. So innocuous. No one could fathom how something so precious, rare, and beautiful could bring an entire world to its pinnacle and then raze it to ashes. But thus is the way of magic. It all comes with a price, and simple as Blue Frost might seem, its price was far greater than any could have imagined.

A wizard discovered it one frigid morning on the first day of winter. It sparkled, instantly drawing him to it, a shimmering shadow against the pearly backdrop of fresh snow. Enthralled, he watched it for hours as it grew on the surface of a remote river. But when he tried to gather some for further study, the heat of his hands melted the bit he'd touched. To his dismay, the heat then radiated out, destroying all the remaining crystals. The wizard left it, disgusted. What could he do with a magic that couldn't be harvested?

Years passed before another being stumbled upon that same river on the first day of winter, this time a sorcerer. Recognizing its potential, he left the strange frost alone, observing from a distance, watching as the deep blue, opalescent crystals grew to wondrous proportions. But as the moon began to wane, so did the crystals. They decayed, becoming nothing but iridescent dust that glinted in the first light of dawn. Then that, too, diminished. The sorcerer left it, saddened. How could he utilize something so short-lived?

More time passed before Blue Frost's third and most important discovery. A child, having heard stories of wizards and sorcerers and the mysterious Blue Frost, sought the river and found it on the first day of winter. The child didn't touch it, fearful he'd destroy it just as the wizard had. But when the sun set and the moon rose, he noticed something the sorcerer hadn't. The crystals of the frost had hardened under the gentle brush of the moon's rays. That night, for the first time, Blue Frost was harvested.

Freed from the river, it did not decay when the moon set and the new dawn rose. The child kept his piece of magic secret, and the next year, he returned to harvest more. That night, he quickly learned how very little time there was to chip away at the crystals. Once the sun set and the moon rose, the crystals continued to solidify, eventually growing so hard they couldn't be broken, and he was forced to leave them to decay.

The next year, he brought a friend and together they worked to gather as many crystals as they could. The year after, others joined them. Each took a few crystals with them, and each vowed to return again on the next first day of winter.

In the years that followed, more and more people gathered at the river, waited for the sun to set and the moon to rise. They took up their picks and blades and plunged them to the frost, chipping away chunks at a time until the river was clear.

Some kept their prizes for decorative purposes; no other stone or gem could equal the beauty of the crystals. Some gathered as much as possible in order to sell it to those who could not make the journey to the river. Some gathered what they could in order to study the frost, what it was, how it formed, why it only formed on one day and why it only decayed if still a part of the river.

Those of magic also gathered what they could. Every year, they made the pilgrimage and every year they learned a little more of what Blue Frost was and what it meant to their gifts, concoctions, enchantments, and spells. Many studied it for its benefits. Others, however, had darker purposes in mind.

Past Tense
(It did happen, it happened, it has happened)

Past Tense is the most used tense in fiction writing. Because of this, readers are most familiar with it. This, however, doesn't mean that it absolutely must be used.

Past Tense allows a certain degree of flow and quite a bit of freedom for world building, backstory, etc., but it also has the potential to lose a degree of immediacy. All stories written in Past Tense are, in essence, being relayed to the reader as if they've already happened. Thus, the narrator of the story (whatever POV chosen) already knows the outcome.

Sometimes it's best to go with the tried, true, and familiar. It's tried, true, and familiar for a reason. On the other hand, it's also good to branch out and experiment. It all depends upon the whims of the writer, the needs of the reader, and what will suit the story best.

COMPARATIVE EXAMPLE OF PAST TENSE:

They couldn't see the ugliness I saw. Their proverbial veils blinded them from the truth. It was a willing ignorance, one I'd never truly known the comfort of. Invisible shields were for those who did not have the strength to face the horrors that haunted the deep recesses of the world. I had that strength. And thus, I had my calling. It was my destiny.

Present Tense
(It happens, it is happening)

As it grows in popularity in modern literature, Present Tense also grows less jarring to the reader who is, for the most part, accustomed to the more recognized Past Tense.

Present Tense is most often associated with First Person, though this is by no means a rule. Present Tense tells the story in the here and now, as if it is unfolding instantaneously. Which means it is an excellent method of adding immediacy and tension to a story. Unlike Past Tense, the narrator in Present Tense doesn't know what will happen next and thus carries the reader along with them as events unfold.

Writers beware, though; Present Tense doesn't offer much opportunity for world building. Immediacy is only exciting as long as it doesn't involve the mundane, and sometimes world building involves mundane/everyday life events.

COMPARATIVE EXAMPLE OF PRESENT TENSE:

They can't see the ugliness I see. Their proverbial veils blind them from the truth. It's a willing ignorance, one I've never truly known the comfort of. Invisible shields are for those who do not have the strength to face the horrors that haunt the deep recesses of the world. I have that strength. And thus, I have my calling. It is my destiny.

Future Tense
(It will happen)

Future Tense is perhaps the most difficult tense to both write and read, and it is not often used as a primary tense.

However, Future Tense is prevalent throughout fiction in smaller doses tucked within either Past or Present Tense stories. Like Second Person POV, Future Tense is often used for prophecy, foretelling, prediction.

Interjections of Future Tense can also be used as a foreshadowing tool in order to build tension regarding future events within the story. This is because the narrator telling the story knows the outcome already and thus offers snippets of what comes ahead as a means of drawing the reader deeper in.

COMPARATIVE EXAMPLE OF FUTURE TENSE:

They'll not see the ugliness I'll see. Their proverbial veils will blind them from the truth. It's a willing ignorance, one I'll never truly know the comfort of. Invisible shields will be for those who don't have the strength to face the horrors that will haunt the deep recesses of the world. I will have that strength. And thus, I will have my calling. It will be my destiny.

Examples of Future Tense Foreshadowing:

Combined with Past Tense, Third Person Expanded

The argument ended when Juliana turned around and softly closed the door behind her, her tears under control until the latch clicked. Richard walked back into the bedroom, all hope lost of ever seeing her again. Not after what he'd just said.

Yet, the future holds a great many mysteries. Juliana will one day return to Breaker House, though she will be much changed by then. Changed in ways Richard couldn't possibly fathom. And so will he.

Combined with Present Tense, First Person

Tears fill my eyes as a deafening roar rises from the army of light. Together, we watch the Master of Dark shrivel into nothingness at my feet, the gloom that once radiated from him now washing away in the growing dawn. The army behind me drowns out the cries of fear and despair from the other side of the battlefield. Yet, I cannot join my comrades in their celebration.

To my shame, they cheer in vain. Though I defeated him, the Master has not perished. My strength wasn't enough. I've only banished him back to the darkness from which he came.

He will rise again, his strength renewed, his lust for darkness tenfold. Even now, even as the last tendrils of shadow diminish before me, my prophetic gifts rob me of any joy. But not of hope.

In my mind, I watch the terror of his second rising unfurl. He will ravage the world and all love and light will be lost. Only then, when the world writhes in the throes of horror and blackness, will a hero rise up.

He will be born into the darkness, a child who knows nothing more than the black, scorched world left in the wake of the Master. But he will grow strong and powerful. He will surpass even me. And when he is strong enough and powerful enough, he will face the Master on a field similar to this one. And he will defeat the darkness once and for all.

The shame I carry with me from my failure this day will haunt me in those years before the instrument of my redemption is born. I will bear witness to everything the Master does to this world, knowing I could have stopped him today but didn't have the strength. But I will live to see the day the darkness is at last conquered. I will live to see the Master draw his last breath in this world. And on that day, then and only then will I truly be free.

Protagonist POV

The Protagonist is the hero of the story. They are the character the reader connects with throughout the story, the character the reader wills and hopes to succeed, and the primary character who accomplishes the story's goal(s) by overcoming the story's underlying conflict(s).

While many readers love a good, virtuous hero to cheer on, anti-heroes are also growing in popularity in modern fiction. Anti-heroes are often perceived as more rounded or realistic due to their extreme flaws and their reluctance to do right without recompense, whether it be monetary or otherwise.

Anti-heroes will always ask the question, *"What's in it for me?"* They are often unwilling to set out and accomplish the story goal and/or overcome the story conflict without due cause, and more often than not, an anti-hero will be coerced, forced, or in rare instances, convinced to do the right thing and take on the role of hero.

To create a realistic hero, however, one does not need to make them utterly flawed, as with the anti-hero. All well-rounded heroes possess both good and bad traits.

Often times part of the story's conflict and goals revolve around the Protagonist overcoming their own personal flaws. These particular flaws almost always become an obstacle to the completion of the story's primary goal and hinder the character from overcoming the story's primary conflict.

When a Protagonist overcomes their personal flaws, it is referred to as *character growth.*

Possible Protagonist Flaws to Overcome:
- ⚔ Fears / Phobias (both rational and irrational)
- ⚔ Insecurities
- ⚔ Mental Illnesses / Psychological Disorders
- ⚔ Cognitive Disabilities
- ⚔ Vices (arrogant, greedy, lazy, short-tempered, self-depreciative, faint-hearted, etc.)
- ⚔ Post Traumatic Stress Disorder
- ⚔ Injuries / Disabilities / Deformities / Health Issues
- ⚔ Undesirable Responses / Tics / Compulsions
- ⚔ Habits / Addictions / Obsessions

Antagonist POV

The Antagonist is the villain of the story, the character who strives to keep the Protagonist from achieving their goals. Typically, the Antagonist is the hero of his own story and views the hero as the villain—they see the hero as the person trying to keep them from their goals.

Just like with the hero, a well-rounded villain will have both good and bad traits. While a hero might strive to overcome his bad traits for the sake of his goals, a villain might be compelled to do the same only in reverse—to overcome his good traits for the sake of his goals.

Just as there are anti-heroes, there can also be anti-villains. Anti-villains still do wrong and are still the "bad guys" of the story. They differ from the traditional villain due to their motivations. Most Anti-villains do wrong for one of three reasons: they're delusional, they're being coerced, or they feel they have no choice.

AN ANTI-VILLAIN COULD BE:

- Someone who truly strives to do what they believe is right without realizing (or willingly acknowledging) that it is in fact wrong.
- Someone who has no choice but to act in the wrong due to outside influences or coercion.
- Someone who must do something they know is wrong in order to achieve the ultimate goal of what they believe is right.

CHALLENGE GLOSSARY

For the anti-villain, the ends almost always justify the means, regardless of how horrific those means might be. In other words, the reasons are always worth the results.

EXAMPLES OF ANTI-VILLAINS:

- ⚔ A king trying to eliminate all forms of magic because he sees magic as corrupt, regardless of the fact that he must massacre sentient magical creatures in order to achieve his goals. (He doesn't see what he's doing is wrong—by his logic, all magic is corrupt and thus if the creatures are magic, then they too are corrupt and must be destroyed.)

- ⚔ A dragon is forced to burn a village because another antagonist has control over her eggs and will destroy them if she doesn't do as told. (She has absolutely no choice but to act in the wrong on another's behalf—kill the villagers, or let her children perish.)

- ⚔ A peasant holds the court healers and their families hostage until the peasant's wife gets the life-saving treatment denied her because of their social standing. (He knows it's wrong to threaten other people's lives, but he feels he has no choice. Despite putting others in danger, he's trying to save the life of the woman he loves.)

HELPING HANDS

Still not a how-to book.

Here you won't find tutorials. You'll find ideas.
You won't find step-by-step instructions. You'll
find suggestions, thoughts, and strategies, each
one designed to coax the elusive muse from
hiding and to guide you in the next step beyond
mere practice.

How and whether you apply them is up to you.

Breaking the Block
Part 1 - Stimulating the Senses

Writer's block has many different forms. Sometimes it's the inability to write or focus due to outside stresses or distractions. Sometimes it occurs when a writer doesn't know what direction they should take a story or what to write next. Sometimes it is a deep-seated fear, the possibility of failure too overwhelming for the creative self. And sometimes, it's when the creative juices are stifled, stuck, or just not flowing.

Though these are just a handful of the many facets of writer's block, this first installment of Breaking the Block will primarily focus on the last one.

DENY IT BATTLE

Sometimes, a writer's creative side will hide. Not just playfully under the desk or behind the curtains of the mind. Sometimes, creativity is elusive, hunkered down into the trenches of the deep psyche, determined not show itself. Drawing it out becomes a battle, and that battle often saps all creative energy before words even touch the page.

One method for overcoming this type of writer's block is to deny it battle in the first place. Fighting to compel the creativity out is exhausting, frustrating, and often times unsuccessful. In those cases, one might consider coaxing creativity instead of forcing it.

One attracts insects with honey rather than vinegar. In the same way, one might attract creativity through sensory experiences rather than by trying to compel it.

Coaxing focuses on the positive rather than the negative. It encourages rather than demands. One way to do this is to focus solely on stimulating the senses. Forget the writing. Forget the story. Just focus on being.

This might seem counter-intuitive—breaking out of writer's block by not writing. However, by stimulating the senses, one stimulates the very things that inspire creativity.

More than Five Senses

The basic definition of a sense is: A means of perceiving. However one perceives the world is determined by how they are able to sense it. For some, this involves any combination of the basic five senses: hearing, sight, smell, taste, and/or touch. These five are the most recognized, but they're not the only ones that exist. For the creative soul, it is important that they're not the only ones to be considered when both experiencing life and while writing about it.

Some studies consider the abilities to sense temperature, pressure, and pain as separate entities from the five senses above. Others regard them as included in the sense of touch. Either which way, for the sake of sensory stimulation, it's important to both remember and recognize their existence.

Other Senses to Take into Account Include:

- The ability to sense magnetic or electric fields.
- The ability to sense bodily needs such as hunger, thirst, lack of oxygen, self-preservation, etc.

- The ability to sense physical space in relation to the body.
- The ability to sense parts of the body in relation to other parts of the body.
- The ability to sense balance and equilibrium, or the lack thereof.
- The ability to sense the passing of time.

BEYOND THE PHYSICAL

All the above senses have one thing in common—they're all physical senses (with perhaps the exception of the last one, which could be both physical and psychological). We sense each and every one of them with our corporeal self. But what about the non-physical senses? Humans are more than just brains and nerves, eyes, ears, mouths, and noses. They are creatures of the psyche as well.

Often, the internal senses are overlooked. Sometimes they're disputed or disparaged. But, for the sake of living and writing, they are no less important than the ones that can be quantified physically.

Non-Physical Senses:
- The sense of emotion: the ability to feel and recognize emotions within the self, as well as the ability to recognize (and sometimes feel) those within others.
- The sense of intuition: the ability to know or understand without direct deliberation or inference, such as gut feelings, hunches, inklings, and insights.
- The senses of sympathy and empathy: the ability to experience other people's experiences vicariously.
- The sense of the spirit: peace, turmoil, and the sensations associated with acknowledging the existence of

a higher being (or beings) and/or higher planes of existence.

⚔ The sense of ego: the sense of the self, the mind, and existential recognition

⚔ The sense of morality: the moral compass that allows one to know right from wrong, good from bad, etc.

⚔ The sense of mortality: an awareness of one's temporal existence, the provisional nature of life, and the gradually deteriorating condition of the physical body

COAXING THE CREATIVE SELF

All the senses mentioned above, and perhaps some not mentioned, are vastly important to any creative individual. How one perceives the world directly reflects upon how they express themselves creatively. Senses are experiences, and the very fuel for the written word is experience.

By embracing the senses, the writer gleans more experience regarding those senses that they can then translate to the page in order to share with the reader. And since readers experience similar means of perception, they can then relate to what the writer has written.

It is this deeper shared translation from writer to reader that makes sensory experience one of the base ingredients to the Show rather than Tell aspect of writing. But how does one go about stimulating their senses?

THE PROCESS OF STIMULATION

In order to stimulate their senses, the writer must first learn to acknowledge them, focus on them, encourage them, and above all else, embrace them.

Acknowledgement begins with simply recognizing the existence of one's senses. Easy enough—all one has to do is look at the lists above (or any list of senses, for that matter) and determine which senses (if not all of them) apply to their own life and experiences.

Focus is a type of internal awareness and is very important to the process. Without that awareness, one cannot fully translate the sensory experience from experience to creative outlet. The more aware a person is of what they're experiencing and how, the more they reap from the experience, and thus the more they're able to share.

If writers—and all they express—are merely the sum of their experiences, then the greater amount of experiences one has, the more they can translate to the page in one way, shape, or form or another. This is the key element to coaxing the creative self out of hiding.

The more a writer encourages experiences with focused awareness, the more they'll able to add to their creative arsenal. When one encourages a vast variety of experiences, they're adding to the pool of thoughts, emotions, ideas, actions, reactions, and senses one must draw from in order to create.

NOT ALL SENSORY EXPERIENCES ARE TREATED EQUAL

People don't always have good sensory experiences. One might get nauseous from the sickening sweet smell of rotting food. Or one might suddenly open their eyes to far too bright of a light. How often do people smack their funny bones on a door jam? How often must a person endure nails on a chalkboard or the ever-constant splat of a leaky faucet?

Pain and discomfort are just as powerful tools as pleasure. In order to truly encourage the creative self, one must learn to embrace all sensory experiences, not just the good, pleasant, or even neutral.

Our characters, those we transfer our experiences upon, don't always get to live happy, pleasant experiences. In fact, most stories thrive on the conflict inflicted upon characters. Negative experiences are just as important as positive ones, if not more so. How can one show their character suffering if they do not know what it is to suffer?

EMBRACING SENSORY EXPERIENCES

To truly embrace sensory experiences, one must not just encourage them and/or focus their awareness upon them. One must also do so with the intent of extracting all possible applications one can employ in their craft from the experience. Embracing equals purpose.

The oft-elusive creative side is attracted to purpose. It can't help but wonder how a character would react to the sudden shattering crash of thunder directly overhead. It can't help but create a situation where several characters are forced to endure the rotten-egg smell of natural gas and the sudden, uncertain fear that particular smell awakens deep within the psyche. It can't help but revel in the thought of a world whose entire society is built upon the concept of gourmet food and dry turkey is a punishable offense.

By intentionally stimulating one's senses—by seeking out and/or focusing one's awareness upon experiences—one grows as a writer, encourages the creative self, and often sparks something that will eventually flow upon the page.

Thus the writer must never take any experience for granted. They must soak everything in with the awareness of how they can translate what they're feeling, seeing, smelling, etc. to the page. They must notice what they've never noticed before, searching for differences, clinging to the new or unusual, feeling keenly each moment in order to better harvest thoughts, ideas, and all the bits and pieces that makes fiction come alive.

By stimulating the senses and embracing the effects, the writer's creative side will grow curious. It will question. It will expand upon flavors, sights, sounds, smells, feelings, emotions, and ideas.

Sensory experience is the basal form of all writer fuel, and sometimes the best way to coax the creative side out of hiding is to simply feed it.

What Now?
Part 1 - The Art of Prompt Maturation

FROM PRACTICE TO INSPIRATION

One of the rewards of regular practice is the myriad of stories, scenes, snippets, and ideas that are generated during practice. Oftentimes those bits and pieces spark something within the creative soul. Sometimes that spark grows into a full-blown blaze. It is in these moments that prompts have the potential to become something far grander than mere practice. They become inspiration.

Prompts can spark complex concepts. Or they can instigate unusual character personalities. They can define situations. Or show a whole new world worthy of exploration. They can offer up new plots, subplots, themes, ideals, and styles. They can reveal endings begging for beginnings and middles to be developed. Or they can do all the above all at once. There is no end to what prompts might inspire because there is no end to the imagination.

But prompt practices as they are cannot stand all on their own. They must be transformed, taken from the basic scribbles of practice sessions to something grander, greater, and altogether stronger. No matter how well one writes during practice, a first draft is never a final one. Thus, one must consider what it means to take their inspiration to the next level and the means of getting it there.

RECOGNIZING THE POTENTIAL

When the spark ignites within the creative soul, when a prompt begs to be transformed, it often reveals the potential for one of three things:

- ⚐ The prompt can be expanded upon to become its own story.
- ⚐ The prompt can be added to an already existing project or idea.
- ⚐ The prompt can be combined with other prompts in order to grow or complete an idea.

Expansion

When a prompt begs to be expanded upon, it means that there is a full story (beginning, middle, and end) hidden deep within it. Sometimes, the basics are all there but need to be fleshed out. Sometimes, beginnings, middles, and/or ends need to be added. Sometimes the prompt is just an idea for a story and thus the story itself has yet to be written. Either which way, the prompt has the potential to become an entire story on it's own with no help from outside inspirations.

Addition

Creative minds often lean towards current projects, themes, or ideas, regardless of whether intended or not. Because of this, a prompt will often express parallels to current non-prompt related pieces. Perhaps it's a character with similar traits. Perhaps it's a setting that strikes a familiar chord. Or even just the basics of a theme. In these cases, it might behoove a writer to take the similar prompt and alter it enough to fit in with the current project. Or alter the current project to include the prompt.

Combination

Though a writer may strive to create something entirely unique with each prompt practice, they may begin to see certain themes and patterns emerge in their writing, regardless of any conscious or unconscious efforts to the contrary. Some parts of the soul cannot be denied, and if a writer finds reoccurring ideas and themes inadvertently popping up in their work, perhaps they should take heed. Perhaps they should consider finding ways to combine the similar prompts into one cohesive idea or project.

THREE MEANS, THREE METHODS, INFINITE POSSIBILITIES

How to proceed depends entirely upon the writer's core type—whether they are a "Pantser" (someone who writes by the seat of their pants), a "Planner" (someone who plans out a story entirely via notes and outlines before writing it), or a Plantser (any combination of the two).

No matter whether a prompt becomes something on its own, is added to something already established, or pieced together with other prompts, each of the above types of writers will proceed differently.

Pantsers

Some writers choose to embrace chaos and uncertainty. For these writers, the Pantsers, the journey is all about the perpetual growth and discovery as it happens. This gives them the opportunity to both focus on the art of writing and the development of a story all at once rather than in separate stages.

Pantsers thrive best when free-writing and find the pre-established structure of the Planners stifling. They like to let their characters run free and evolve, forming the story around their actions and reactions, whatever they may be in the moment.

When it comes to converting prompts into something more, one of the common methods Pantsers employ is simply treating the entire prompt text as a new prompt in and of itself. They do this by using it as inspiration to create a whole new piece. Another method they may consider is to attempt a full rewrite of the original prompt, this time adding, cutting, and/or tweaking bits and pieces as they go. Or, perhaps they might merely continue where the prompt left off. Either way, the best means for a Pantser to expand upon a prompt is to simply write and let the story take them where it will.

One of the struggles Pantsers face most often is the "what next" form of writer's block. Sometimes, they just don't know where to take a story from a certain point, and their characters, for one reason or another, have stopped talking to them. Sometimes, they'll reach the middle of a story, realize an entire section isn't working, and have to go back and either fix it or rewrite it to fit the story better as a whole. Because Pantsers tend to wing it, they often face quite a bit of rewriting in order to produce a story that is strong, worthwhile, and complete.

Planners

Unlike Pantsers, Planners thrive on structure and organization. By establishing a story's core elements beforehand, a Planner frees their creative soul to focus entirely on the task at hand. They compartmentalize the various stages of writing

—development, the writing itself, rewriting, etc.—thus allowing them to concentrate their skills and attention on just one stage at a time.

When a Planner sees the potential for a full story hidden within a prompt, one of the first things they'll do is jot down the initial inspiration and any notes, thoughts, ideas, etc. associated with it. Sometimes they'll go through and pick out which pieces of a prompt will need to be kept, enhanced, and/or cut. They may fill out story worksheets that help establish characters, settings, plot and subplot points, areas requiring research, and so on.

More than likely, Planners will then create an outline. The outline could be simple, noting general events and where they happen in the story. It could be complex, marking exactly when and where events will unfold, how they'll unfold, who will be involved, and so on. No matter what a Planner does, they'll always know where they want the idea to go ahead of time, and a great big part of the process is creating the roadmap of how to get there.

Unfortunately, the rigidity of creating such a complete structure before writing a piece can sometimes be just as stifling as the Pantsers' "what next" blockage. Ideas aren't always solidified. More often than not, they evolve. Characters may grow in unexpected directions. Settings may change. New inspirations may alter preconceived notions. And if this happens, all pre-established notes and outlines must be altered accordingly in order to maintain a degree of continuity, thus throwing the Planner back into the planning stage instead of allowing them to continue on in the writing stage.

Another pitfall for Planners is boredom. They know what will happen ahead of time, so there's no adventure for them in the writing stage itself. That adventure of discovery is already over, having happened during the planning process. Thus the actual writing of a story has the potential to become tedious.

Plantsers

Plantsers will always be a combination of the two extremes, creating a working balance of them by both avoiding the rigidity of the Planners while also avoiding the randomness of the Pantsers. They do this by maintaining some form of simple structure to fall back on without that structure being set entirely in stone.

They may jot a few notes as reminders of where they want the story to go and then write freely without an outline. Or they'll put together a simple outline, keeping it fluid so it won't stifle the creative process of seeing where the story might take them. They may create the outline as they write, or keep a notebook with new thoughts, ideas, and inspirations throughout the process. The key to prompt expansion, addition, and combination with Plantsers, is to find the right balance between preparation and free-writing that suits their needs and creative soul best.

One of greatest aspects about being a Plantser is the inherent adaptability. If they find themselves in the toil of "what now" blockage, or if they feel too stifled, or if the story requires more or less development, they can alter their methods with very little difficulty.

However, just like absolute rigidity and absolute randomness, the Plantsers' adaptability has the potential for its own downsides. Often, the complete fluidity of the process makes it difficult to settle down into an established method and maintain a consistent flow. Plantsers experiment the most, trying to find the best combination of the two methods, but in doing so, they run the risk of focusing more on the method than on the writing and/or planning.

Experimentation is Key

There are no right or wrong writing core methods. Each has their strengths and weaknesses, merits and annoyances. Experimentation is key to discovering which of the three core types of writers works best for each individual.

Regardless of what type a writer is, practice is exercise for the muscles of the imagination. And the more one exercises, the stronger they become. Thus, the more prompt practices one writes, the more possibility they'll find inspiration within their own work.

NOT QUITE THE END

Want more prompts, challenges, examples, and helping hands? Did this book inspire you and spark the creative self within? If so, turn the page and discover these other titles in the SpecFicWrit series...

If the Spark Fits...
Other Books in the SpecFicWrit Series

101 FANTASY WRITING PROMPTS
VOLUMES 2 – 4
Each featuring new prompt lists, challenges, and helping hands.
(Available Fall 2015)

101 SCIENCE FICTION WRITING PROMPTS
VOLUMES 1 – 4
Each featuring new prompt lists, challenges, and helping hands.
(Volumes 2-4 available Fall 2015)

101 PARANORMAL WRITING PROMPTS
VOLUMES 1 – 4
Each featuring new prompt lists, challenges, and helping hands.
(Volumes 2-4 available Fall 2015)

Coming Soon...

COLLECTED FANTASY
All four volumes combined, plus 101 additional prompts, 10 new
challenges, and an expanded helping hands section.

COLLECTED SCIENCE FICTION
All four volumes combined, plus 101 additional prompts, 10 new
challenges, and an expanded helping hands section.

COLLECTED PARANORMAL
All four volumes combined, plus 101 additional prompts, 10 new
challenges, and an expanded helping hands section.

SpecFicWrit Epic Writing Prompt Collection

All four volumes of all three genres, all additional material from the three collections, plus 303 additional prompts and 20 bonus challenges exclusive to the Epic Collection

✦ ✦ ✦ ✦ ✦ ✦ ✦

Have questions, suggestions, thoughts, or requests?

Looking for links to the other SpecFicWrit Books above?

Want updates, announcements, new and exclusive prompts, thoughts, ideas, and breakdowns of the writing process?

Please visit and follow SpecFicWrit at:

www.facebook.com/specficwrit

PLEASE NOTE:

Each genre-specific volume in the SPECFICWRIT series mirrors the same numbered volume in the other genres. The introduction, challenges, and helping hands are all virtually the same for Fantasy vol. 1, Science Fiction vol. 1, and Paranormal vol. 1, etc. However, the prompt lists and many examples within the Challenge Glossaries are different, each geared towards their own genres.

If you are interested in all three genres, but don't want as much repetitive text, please consider SPECFICWRIT'S EPIC PROMPT COLLECTION (coming soon) featuring ALL the lists and information within ALL the SPECFICWRIT prompt booklets and collections plus much, much more.

Other Books by J. Dodson

ECHOING SACRIFICE: TRAVELER

Still reeling from the death of her parents, thirteen-year-old Khyl Livingston's entire existence revolves around the care and protection of her brothers. But when an accident strands her in Dolimar, a world populated by both humans and dragons, she finds yet another child in desperate need of protection.

Rever barely survived the slaughter of the Echo Dragons at the hand of the Betrayer. When he meets Khyl, old wounds at last begin to heal, and their growing friendship distracts him from his need for vengeance. But the courageous Traveler couldn't have come at a worse time. The Betrayer returns to Rever's home, this time with an army and the intent to carry out a deadly bargain with the greatest threat in all Dolimar.

Bound by friendship and united in common purpose, Khyl and Rever stand against the Betrayer and his allies in order to save an innocent child from a fate worse than death. Dolimar itself hangs in the balance, and one wrong choice could cost them everything they hold dear.

Including each other.

For links to the books, updates, sneak peeks, and behind the scenes looks into the creation of the
ECHOING SACRIFICE TRILOGY,
part of the GATES OF DOLIMAR BOOK SERIES,
please visit author Jessica NA Dodson at:

www.facebook.com/echoingsacrificetrilogy

ECHOING SACRIFICE: CAPTIVE

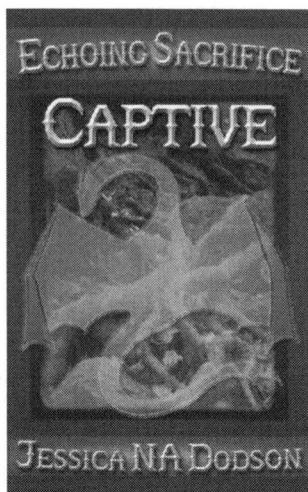

ECHOING SACRIFICE

CAPTIVE

JESSICA N A DODSON

Though Khyl fulfilled her promise to Litha and helped her escape Tumulus' clutches, Dolimar's newest Traveler only now begins to realize the true consequence of her sacrifice back at SallowLake. The EastKeeper is determined to recapture the SouthPrincess at all costs, and to Khyl's horror, the SlaveSpine poison now flowing through her might just be the key to his success.

Rever came dangerously close to his vengeance at SallowLake, and it's all he can do to keep from hunting the Betrayer down and destroying the man who slaughtered his family once and for all. Yet, Khyl needs him now more than ever. Torn between the need to protect his friend and the overwhelming thirst for revenge, Rever risks losing everything to achieve both.

After battling his way past the EastKeeper's minions into the West, King Athius finds no rest, even with the joyful news that his daughter is free. Tumulus' forces converge upon WestFalls Forest, and for the sake of Litha and their new allies, the young King of Ithana has no choice but to mount his army and prepare for war.

With the help of their friends, Khyl, Rever, and Athius face life, death, and everything in between as they strive to rid the West of Tumulus and his brutal allies. All the while, the "great foreboding" hangs over their heads, always threatening to come crashing down upon them.

None more so than Khyl.

About the Author

Jessica N A Dodson has been imagining new worlds since before she can remember and began writing them into stories at the age of eight. Inspired by both the beauty and struggle in everyday life, and passionate about philosophy, she strives to include the power of perseverance, the ideals of betterment, and the message of overcoming all odds into every piece she creates.

A firm believer that practice makes perfect, Dodson began her prompt writing journey over a decade before publishing her first fantasy novel, ECHOING SACRIFICE: TRAVELER, in October 2013. The ideas and skills gleaned during her practice sessions eventually prompted her to create SPECFICWRIT, a series of booklets devoted to developing writing proficiency while specifically focusing on the various aspects of speculative fiction.

She currently lives in her own little world, but when not there she can be found in Colorado with her husband and two dachshunds.

Printed in Great Britain
by Amazon